REVOLUTIONARY PORTRAITS ■ MOZART

Mozart: overture to revolution *Paul McGarr*

First published in *International Socialism* 52, Autumn 1991

This edition published in 2001 by

REDWORDS

1 Bloomsbury Street, London WC1B 3QE

www.redwords.org.uk

ISBN: 1 872208 14 2

Design and production: Roger Huddle

Printed by Interprint Ltd, Malta

Cover: The storming of the Bastille, Paris 1789

Mozart:
overture to revolution

Paul McGarr

Publishers note

This book is one of the first in a major series of **Revolutionary Portraits** from Redwords. The unifying theme in this eclectic collection is Marxism. Each author reviews the artist and their art in historical context. The focus is on the relationship between individual artists and larger historical forces, how each influences and shapes the other. All of the books in this series aim to lead us back to these works of art and music with new eyes and ears and a deeper understanding of how art can raise the human spirit.

Others books in the current series are: Diego Rivera, Rembrandt, and John Coltrane.

Redwords is a publishing collective specialising in art, history and literature from a socialist perspective. We are linked to Bookmarks.

REVOLUTIONARY PORTRAITS

Introduction

Wolfgang Amadeus Mozart's bicentenary in 1991 was marked by an explosion of Mozartmania. Mozart's name, fame and, occasionally, music were being used to sell everything from tea-towels, underwear and chocolates to holidays, books and records.

The image of Mozart presented was that of a romantic caricature. Mozart the child prodigy who, through some preternatural gift, was writing masterpieces while still in nappies. Mozart the individual genius who never had to work at his craft but who composed huge works conceived in a moment of mystical inspiration. Mozart the lone artist, spurned and misunderstood by society, and living his final years in failing health and battling against poverty. Finally, there was the romantic tragedy of one of the greatest artists in history dying a premature death and ending in an unmarked pauper's grave—his true greatness only appreciated by later generations.

There are, as usual, elements of truth buried amid the myths. It is certainly true that the sheer quality and quantity of the work Mozart produced in such a short life are remarkable. But Mozart and his music can only be fully understood, appreciated and explained as part of the changing world that produced them.

Mozart lived in an age of crisis and revolution. He was born in Salzburg, in what is now Austria, in 1756. That year saw the start of the Seven Years War. It was in many ways a new kind of war, the first global conflict, fought out not just in Europe but across the rival empires, stretching from India to the Caribbean and North America, of the world's two major powers— England and France.

By the time Mozart died 35 years later the world had changed beyond recognition under the impact of two of the most important revolutions in history. First came the American Revolution (1775-83) in which the former British colonies won their independence in a revolutionary war. Then came the most decisive event in modern history until 1917—the Great French

Revolution which erupted in 1789. Its impact was to reshape the world for ever.

The ideas of 'liberty, equality and fraternity' were born of the Enlightenment, the great philosophical and cultural movement of the 18th century, centered in France but whose impact was immense across all Europe. The Age of Reason declared by the Enlightenment built on the scientific discoveries of the 17th century and projected a world controlled by people with rational ideas. The major works of key Enlightenment figures such as Voltaire, Diderot, Rousseau, Beccaria and Kant were published during Mozart's life. James Watt patented his steam engine and Adam Smith published his *Wealth of Nations*, which, in their different ways, heralded the new industrial capitalist society then emerging in Britain, as Mozart emerged from his teens.

In music it was a revolutionary age too. New forms which have shaped music ever since were developed. The very label 'classical' music describes a style evolved in the latter half of the 18th century. Composers of the 19th century self-consciously felt themselves working in the shadow of the giants of the 'classical' age—Haydn, Mozart and Beethoven.

REVOLUTIONARY PORTRAITS

A changing society

Mozart's birthplace, Salzburg, was the principal city and residence of a powerful feudal ruler, a prince-archbishop. He was both spiritual and temporal ruler, and the highest ranking archbishop in the Holy Roman Empire which stretched across most of German-speaking Europe from the Baltic to the Alps. The empire consisted of a host of kingdoms, dukedoms, principalities, counties and independent imperial cities woven together in a complex patchwork. The whole ramshackle structure had grown from the old feudal society with its endless dynastic conflicts and wars. With land and the labour to work it the key source of wealth, feudal rulers sought to extend the lands they controlled. The emperor was chosen by the Electors—a small group of some of the most important of the scores of feudal rulers within the empire.

From 1508 until the empire's dissolution in 1806, under the impact of the Napoleonic Wars, all but one of the emperors were members of the Habsburg family which had its seat of power in Vienna, the imperial capital. This family were also hereditary rulers of their own Austrian Empire, some of which was inside the Holy Roman Empire but which also covered areas outside like Hungary. The Habsburgs had been among the most successful of the great feudal rulers of Europe. In Mozart's time, however, the society over which they ruled was changing.

Feudal society had been based on local production and consumption and, therefore, a decentralised political structure. Local lords exploited the majority of the population, who were tied to the land and compelled, by the use or threat of force, to hand over part of their labour or produce. The Catholic church was the key ideological force in this society and a major feudal landowner in its own right. Kings and powerful rulers had to balance the claims of local rulers who had a monopoly of armed force in their own domains. No centralised state was possible. With land the main form of wealth, warfare aimed at the acquisition of land and the labour to work it was endemic.

Feudalism, though not as dynamic as capitalism, was not a totally stagnant system. With the growth of trade and improved production larger regions were knitted together economically and socially. The decentralised political structures meant the towns which developed as centres of trade were able to become relatively independent of local feudal lords. In the towns new classes, political structures and ideas began slowly to develop. The most important of the changes was the emergence of a new class, the bourgeoisie. This class, the ancestor of today's capitalist class, was based at first on trade and later on increasing control of production. As its economic power in society grew, so did its social and political weight.

It also produced the great artistic and cultural movement known as the Renaissance—based, at least in rhetoric, on the rediscovery and then development of the heights of the ancient Greek and Roman civilisations after the Dark Ages of classical feudalism. This movement had its centre in the great cities of northern Italy, then the most advanced and independent of the old feudal structures in Europe.

These changes, and the upheavals they produced, led to a modified form of feudal rule. The key change was the development of centralised absolute monarchies—

absolutism. Economic and social life had begun to outgrow the local horizons of feudalism. This laid the basis for the development of bigger, more unified 'national' economies and states. Absolutism was a partial recognition of this. Kings moved to curb much of the independent power of local feudal rulers and construct a more unified centralised state. Though the local feudal rulers maintained their political domination of society, they were increasingly subordinated to central rulers.

The model absolutist regime was that of Louis XIV in France. The 'Sun King' ruled from his magnificent palace at Versailles outside Paris. The Esterhazy family, for instance, the great feudal lords in Hungary who employed the composer Joseph Haydn, Mozart's long-lived great predecessor and then contemporary, modelled their palace and much else besides on Versailles. So did countless other lesser local rulers across Europe.

Absolutism incorporated elements of the growing bourgeoisie. Significant elements of the bourgeoisie everywhere used their growing wealth to obtain lucrative positions within the growing state bureaucracy. Absolutist rulers came more and more to rely on the wealthy bourgeoisie to bankroll their regimes. The bulk of the bourgeoisie, however, remained excluded from the privileged orders of society. Absolutism was thus an adaptation to and partial incorporation of the bourgeoisie within a reshaped and restabilised feudal political structure. Frederick Engels summed up the situation when he wrote, 'The political order remained feudal while society became more and more bourgeois'.[1]

The trend towards such absolutist regimes was common to almost all of Europe. It wasn't a peaceful or smooth process. In France, for instance, it took the civil wars known as the Wars of Religion in the late 16th century and then another round of civil war called the Frondes in the mid-17th century before the new type of regime was consolidated.

In some countries renewed social and political crises were resolved differently. In two of the most economically advanced parts of Europe, the Netherlands and England, the old feudal order was swept away in revolutionary upheavals and the whole of society decisively reshaped in the interests of the bourgeoisie.

Elsewhere in Europe absolutist regimes were consolidated, particularly in France, Prussia and the Austrian Empire. But the bourgeoisie continued to grow in economic and social power, which caused increasing internal pressures for change. Also the ramshackle feudal structures in the absolutist regimes came under

1 Quoted in P Anderson, *Lineages of the Absolutist State* (London, 1974), p23.

increasing strain as they tried to match, economically and militarily, the new bourgeois regimes in England and Holland.

Reform, revolution and reaction

This combination of internal and external pressures culminated in a series of attempts at reform from above in the mid to late 18th century. The reform programmes which some absolutist rulers attempted to carry through were ideologically underpinned by the thought of the Enlightenment. This is why the label 'enlightened absolutism' has been attached to these regimes—in particular to those of Frederick the Great, ruler of Prussia from 1740 to 1786, and Joseph II, ruler from 1765 to 1790 (at first jointly with his mother, the Empress Maria Theresa) of the Austrian Empire and the Holy Roman Empire.

The roots of the Enlightenment lay in the 16th and 17th century revolution in understanding the world. Central to this was the scientific revolution that culminated in the work of figures like Isaac Newton and the breakdown of the old religious view of the world which had dominated feudal society. The centre of gravity of the Enlightenment was among a group of *philosophes* (the name they gave themselves) in 18th century France. The movement, though, spread far beyond France and became a European-wide phenomenon. The basic theme of the Enlightenment was the attempt to apply rational, scientific principles to social, political and cultural questions. Diderot and D'Alembert produced the multi-volume Encyclopedia, which became the centrepiece of the movement; Voltaire hammered away at the superstitions and irrationalities of the old order; Montesquieu wrote his highly influential *Spirit of the Laws*, advocating a reformed, more rational political order with a balance of powers between king and aristocracy; and the Genevan philosopher Jean Jacques Rousseau produced his *Social Contract*, with its famous opening sentence, 'Man is born free and everywhere he is in chains.'

Many of the Enlightenment *philosophes* were sporadically persecuted by the authorities. Occasionally they were imprisoned, their books sometimes banned and burned. But over the course of the 18th century they gradually battered down the ideological defenses of the old order. The new ideas filtered down through society. The growing social weight of the bourgeoisie was reflected in the new academies, reading societies, public libraries and salons of fashionable society that developed across Europe. These eagerly consumed and spread the ideas of the *philosophes*.

Absolute rulers adopted aspects of Enlightenment thought to justify attempts at reform from above. In essence, their aim was to preserve the core of the existing political structure—above all the monarchy and the absolutist state—while carrying through a reorganisation of society along more bourgeois lines. The trend to 'enlightened' reforms from above was fairly general across much of Europe, but the attempts expressed the contradictory position of rulers caught between a need to liberalise their regimes and the fear that this could spill into revolution from below.

The most determined attempt at reform from above came in the Austrian Empire. Joseph II became co-ruler of the Austrian Empire in 1765. From then until 1780 he ruled alongside his mother, the Empress Maria Theresa. After her death Joseph ruled alone until his own death in 1790. At first slowly, while his mother—who was a far more conservative ruler—was alive, and then at breakneck pace when he ruled alone, Joseph attempted to push through a series of radical changes. It is the development of this attempt at reform from above, and its eventual abandonment and turn to reaction by the regime, that forms the crucial background to Mozart's mature life.

Joseph's central aim was to increase the revenues of the state and to make that state more unified. This entailed a series of attacks on key elements of the old order—in particular the Catholic church and powerful local feudal rulers.

The regime sought not to break the Catholic church. Both Joseph and, especially, Maria Theresa were devout Catholics and understood only too well the important role the church played in maintaining ideological and social order. Rather their aim was to subordinate the church to the state. Joseph curtailed the independent power of the church and the privileges of the clergy. The Jesuits, the ideological shock troops of the Roman church, were a particular target. In 1773 Maria Theresa and Joseph suppressed the order and confiscated its considerable wealth. Monasteries too were an easy and lucrative target. They owned over 10 percent of all land in the Brabant province of the Austrian Netherlands, for instance. Joseph suppressed around 750 monasteries and other religious houses across his domains.

In 1781 Joseph went further with his Tolerance Edict which ended legal discrimination against Protestants and other non-Catholics. He reduced previously strict censorship and curtailed the role of the church in it. He also reformed and rationalised the legal codes in the Habsburg domains by permitting civil marriage, and abolishing the death penalty and torture. The whole education system was overhauled and extended. General schooling was introduced in 1774 and the role of the church in it reduced.

Joseph attempted to promote German, the language of Austria, as the 'national' language of his domains as he tried to weld them together. A new legal code was drawn up in German rather than the traditional Latin. The sponsoring of German extended to the state backing German language theatre and opera. In 1776 he founded the German National Theatre in Vienna, and Mozart's German language operas *Die Entführung aus dem Serail* (*The Abduction from the Harem*, first performed in 1782 in Joseph's Burgtheater) and *Die Zauberflöte* (*The Magic Flute*, 1791) are perhaps the first major German language operas.

Joseph sought above all to increase the revenues of the state. A large part of this need came from the demands of war. The Austrian standing army was maintained at a then astonishingly high size of around 200,000 throughout the 1780s. It expanded to a vast 315,000 in the 1788-90 war between Austria and the great Eastern power of the Turkish Empire. Joseph's aim to boost state revenues led him to push through a series of attacks on local feudal rulers. With the bulk of the population peasants, and in most cases serfs, the only way to substantially increase central revenue was to divert a portion of the wealth the peasants produced away from local rulers and towards the state instead.

This, along with an attempt to make peasants more productive, lay behind a series of moves which began to free serfs from the land, limit how much a peasant had to pay to a local lord, and attack various feudal restrictions on land ownership throughout the Habsburg Empire. It also lay behind limitations on *robot*, compulsory labour peasants had to perform for feudal lords.

Peasants gained some benefits, and local feudal lords lost out badly in many areas. But peasants still had to hand over between 40 and 50 percent of their income in Austria, Bohemia and Moravia, for instance. The peasants' situation remained harsh—around 250,000 died of hunger in Bohemia after a series of poor harvests in the early 1770s. There were repeated and major peasant revolts which Joseph the 'enlightened' ruler was more than willing to brutally suppress by force, as in Bohemia in 1775 and Transylvania in 1784.

Throughout the 1770s and especially the early 1780s Joseph carried on the reforms at breakneck speed. These reforms created a much more open and radical cultural and intellectual climate, especially in the great cities of the empire such as Vienna and Prague, than in most other places in Europe. Reform and attempted restructuring of society from above, against the opposition of powerful sections of the existing order, necessitated a freer intellectual and cultural licence. Joseph needed at least to have urban, 'enlightened' bourgeois support for his programme to counter the opposition he was stoking up elsewhere.

That opposition eventually culminated in crisis and revolt in several parts of the empire. In Hungary nobles resentful of Joseph's attacks on their privileges and language rights took advantage of the military failures of the Austrian regime in the war with Turkey. They increasingly defied the Habsburg regime and in 1789 openly revolted. The increased taxation and army recruitment drive provoked by the Turkish wars also led to growing resentment at Joseph's regime among the mass of ordinary people throughout the empire. In the Austrian Netherlands (Belgium) Joseph's reforms had been badly received, but he pushed ahead nonetheless. In 1789 major tax changes were imposed. A powerful protest movement, including riots, had forced the local authorities in Brussels to rescind some of the earlier changes. But resistance to the 1789 decrees was met by the use of troops. The move provoked open rebellion and a successful rising which culminated in the proclamation of a Belgian republic in January 1790.

But the event that led to the complete abandonment of Joseph's reforms and a decisive turn to reaction was the electric shock of the news from France in 1789—revolution. The storming of the Bastille in July, the formation of the National Assembly, and then, in August, the abolition of feudal rights and privileges struck fear into the hearts of rulers across Europe. The spectre of revolution issuing from the opposition and resistance to their own regimes suddenly loomed large. The fear was brought more sharply home to Joseph than most. Marie Antoinette, the French queen on the receiving end of the revolution, was his sister. Also the news from Paris was received with delight by many of the most enthusiastic backers of reform in Vienna.

A British diplomat was present when Joseph heard of the storming of the Bastille: 'It excited a transport of passion, and drew from him the most violent menaces of vengeance'.[2] Three months later the French king, Louis XVI, and Marie Antoinette were forcibly removed from their palace at Versailles by another armed rising and carried back to Paris with the heads of two of their personal guards carried on pikes in the procession.

2 Quoted in A Steptoe, 'Enlightenment and Revolution', in H C Robbins Landon (ed), *The Mozart Compendium: A Guide to Mozart's Life and Music* (London, 1990), p68.

The effects of the French Revolution in the Habsburg Empire were dramatic and swift. Within months Joseph reversed the reform policies he had been pursuing for decades. When revolution threatened, the enlightened absolutist ruler ditched the Enlightenment and clung to absolutism. Censorship was reimposed and a strengthened police force built to enforce control. Newspapers were suppressed, and people thought to be subversive were rounded up and detained without trial. Freemasonry, which had provided many of the key backers of Joseph's reforms, was also suppressed. The relative intellectual and cultural freedom which had marked Vienna for much of the 1780s vanished in the freezing gale of full-blown reaction.

Mozart's mature life was spent in Vienna in the heady years of Joseph's reforms and the subsequent reaction. The whole of his mature life and work cannot be understood without placing it in that context. Mozart settled permanently in Vienna in 1781, the year after Joseph became sole ruler of the empire. He died ten years later, shortly after the would-be enlightened ruler and his reforms had also met their end.

Freemasonry

Freemasonry today is a wholly reactionary gathering of corrupt policemen, businessmen and politicians greasing each other's palms behind a veil of secrecy. It was not always so. In the 18th century Freemasonry stood in the camp of reform and progress against reaction and the worst aspects of existing society. Mozart was an active Freemason. Much of his music and one of the greatest of his operas are intimately concerned with the ideas of Masonry.

Freemasonry began in Britain, where the Grand Lodge of England was founded in 1717. That its birth should come in England, where the bourgeoisie was firmly entrenched in power, is no surprise. Freemasonry was basically a movement which reflected (albeit in an often confused way) the developing consciousness and ideology of the bourgeoisie.

From England it spread rapidly throughout the continent and drew in those who had at least some commitment, however vague or rhetorical, to a more rational, enlightened world. The membership of the Masonic lodges included many from the existing ruling order, including reforming rulers like Frederick the Great of Prussia and countless nobles across Europe. But its core membership and certainly its ideas were of the bourgeoisie. Many of the great *philosophes* of the Enlightenment were also Masons—Voltaire, Montesquieu and Helvetius, for instance. It would be a mistake to see all Masonic lodges and their members as active in any political sense. Often they were little more than social clubs with strange rituals. But many did articulate and push for decidedly reformist, and in some cases revolutionary, demands. In France many of the future leaders of the revolution cut their teeth in Masonic lodges or various societies which were offshoots of Masonry.

The Masons drew on the rituals and symbols of medieval guilds. But they promoted ideas which clashed with the established order of political absolutism and religious orthodoxy imposed by a state church. A cult of reason was at the centre of much Masonic ritual and thought. They stood against the arbitrary and irrational nature of chunks of the existing order and its ideology.

The Masons therefore soon clashed with the Catholic church, the bastion of reaction throughout Europe, though many Masons remained Catholics. In 1738 Pope Clement XII condemned the Masons, and in states like Spain, Portugal, much of Italy and Bavaria, where the grip of the Catholic church was strong, Masonry made little headway. In the Habsburg Empire the situation was different. In large measure this derived from Joseph's need to mobilise pro-reform forces behind his regime. Joseph differed from his mother and long time co-ruler, Maria Theresa, on the approach to the Masons. In 1777 Kaunitz, head of the empire's day to day government, moved to take action against Masonic lodges in the Austrian Netherlands. Joseph defended the Masons: 'Their innocence is recognised by all sensible persons in society'.[3] Maria Theresa nonetheless subsequently sought to suppress Masonic lodges. Her anti-Masonic reputation was to find expression in the character of the Queen of the Night in Mozart's opera *The Magic Flute*.

When Joseph became sole ruler in 1780 and set about his reform programme, he encouraged the Masons, who became his most enthusiastic backers. This association of Masonry with radical change alarmed many rulers. The rulers of Bavaria, Austria's neighbour, denounced the Masons as tools of that dangerous reformer Joseph plotting to take over their state. They reserved particular venom for an offshoot of the Masons called the Illuminati. The Illuminati were founded in 1776 by Adam Weishaupt, an academic in Ingolstadt University in Bavaria, in order to 'help reason gain supremacy'.[4] In 1785 they and all Masonic lodges were

3 J Black, *Eighteenth Century Europe* (London 1990), p399.
4 Ibid.

banned in Bavaria. The government denounced 'that abominable sect, which directly seeks to destroy religion and healthy morals, and to overthrow the thrones of rulers'.[5] In Austria the Masons were highly influential as long as Joseph's reforms were pushing ahead. They were suppressed when those reforms were reversed in the face of the French Revolution.

Mozart flirted with Masonry before he settled in Vienna in 1781. But after his move there he became a member. So did his father, as well as his fellow composer Joseph Haydn. Mozart was acquainted with the various Masonic lodges in Vienna and their differing ideas and emphases. He chose to join two of the most pro-reform lodges—Beneficence and True Concord. Mozart at one time proposed, even if only half seriously, to set up his own Masonic-type organisation called the Grotto, a name derived from the works of Rousseau. He was also influenced by a radical Masonic thinker called Zeigenhagen, who advocated equality for men and women. Women were excluded from full membership of Masonic lodges, though in some countries they were allowed a kind of associate membership. Many Masonic lodges were extremely anti-women in their ideas. Mozart was to caricature this attitude and come down firmly on the side of women being allowed to be members in his *Magic Flute*. But before discussing this and the rest of Mozart's work, some general discussion of the place and role of music and musicians in the society of Mozart's day would be useful.

Music, musicians and society

The 18th century saw a transformation in the social role of music and musicians. At the time of Mozart's birth music was still largely dominated by court and church across most of Europe. Religious music was the dominant form of music at the start of the century. By the end of the century, for the first time in the Christian era in Europe, secular music had completely outstripped sacred music in importance and volume of production.

Musicians in the 18th century were usually servants fairly low in the pecking order in an aristocratic or ecclesiastical court. They were somewhere below the status of the cook and above that of a valet. Independent musicians were a rare, almost non-existent breed. The only few who with any consistency managed to live not tied as servants to a particular court were the most successful opera composers who travelled Europe working on commissions in the great opera houses, or the most virtuoso instrumentalists earning money from giving

6 A Steptoe, 'Patronage and the Place of the Musician in Society', in H C Robbins Landon (ed) op cit, p69.

concerts and lessons. But these were exceptions. The great and even then famous composer Haydn was for most of his life a feudal servant on the estates of the Esterhazy family in Hungary. He was obliged to wear a servant's uniform throughout his career there and not allowed to travel without his lord's permission. Musicians were often expected to do other menial duties. An advert in the 1790s in a Vienna newspaper read:

A musician is wanted who plays the piano well and can sing too, and is able to give lessons in both. This musician must also perform the duties of a valet-de-chambre.[6]

The great courts had large musical establishments which each local ruler or would-be ruler sought to imitate on a smaller scale. Musicians who were also composers (and the distinction between performer and composer was not as clear as it has become today) had to write to order for a whole series of occasions. Operas, masques, masses and other works for the entertainment or worship of the aristocracy were demanded. So were dances and what was basically background music to be played as an amusing diversion during or after dinner in the great houses. Though church music became relatively less important during the century it remained, at least in Catholic countries, an important demand on composers.

But the changing world was opening new

opportunities. Above all, the growing bourgeoisie formed an increasingly wealthy and important audience and market, especially in the major cities like London, Paris and Vienna. This growing bourgeoisie began demanding music of its own which took the form of an increase in concerts in public halls, rather than simply in the mansions, churches and houses of the aristocracy. There was also an increasing demand for music for bourgeois social occasions—dances, balls and serenades.

Much of the music of Mozart and his contemporaries was written under orders for specific occasions by both the old and new audience. The idea of a composer writing from inspiration and for some higher artistic purpose fits ill with the social reality of Mozart's day. Musicians and composers had to, and expected to, produce quickly when told to do so by their masters or those paying their fees.

Some musical accomplishment was fashionable among the aristocracy, and soon became so among wider layers of the bourgeoisie. Live music was the principal form of entertainment in both social and domestic settings. Women in particular were expected to play the keyboard and sing, but so were men. Many bourgeois became reasonably accomplished amateur musicians. This encouraged professional musicians to write and publish for sale works capable of being played by these amateurs. The bulk of this music was for the instruments bought and used in these circles. This meant a growth in music for keyboards of various types from harpsichords to pianos, and the development of small-scale combinations of stringed instruments. The growing popularity of the relatively expensive keyboard reflected the increasing wealth of wide layers of the bourgeoisie. A budding composer usually announced their arrival with a simple set of solo keyboard pieces (often labeled sonatas) designed to be played in domestic settings by amateur players. Mozart's earliest published works, for example, were solo sonatas for piano and violin designed for this kind of audience.

All this in turn spawned an explosion of music copying which was often done by hand due to the limitations and cost of printing techniques. The philosopher Rousseau, for example, scraped by in hard times by doing such music copying. For the first time in history written music became widely available and individual composers could acquire an audience, or 'public'. The performing amateur would also pay to hear great virtuosi playing, which increased the possibility and demand for such performances.

All these developments were fed by and themselves

fuelled rapid technical advances in musical instruments which were to change the kind of music possible. The most important such innovation of the 18th century was the introduction of the piano—possession of which soon became a status symbol for the bourgeoisie.

The piano was developed from the cembalo or harpsichord, in which jacks pluck strings to produce musical notes. In around 1700 an instrument maker in Florence called Cristofori inserted hammers to strike rather than pluck the strings. He called the new instrument the *cembalo col pian'e forte*, which rapidly became known as the pianoforte (from the Italian for quiet and loud), and finally simply the piano. The name derives from the fact that the advantage of the hammers is that the relative loudness of any note can be controlled by the player. The musical possibilities of the piano are much greater than previous keyboard instruments. By the 1790s the piano had more or less supplanted the harpsichord. This technical development opened the possibility for composers to begin to write a new kind of music. Mozart was perhaps the first great composer to write for the piano and developed a range of music new in its day, which even now has rarely been equalled.

Technical developments and limitations had profound effects on all aspects of music composition and performance. Only in the 1780s did the general use of different groups of wind instruments become common in most orchestras. Before then the standard orchestra had generally been composed of stringed instruments and a continuo (usually a harpsichord). Particular problems were the technical difficulties on wind and brass instruments which meant the tonal range was limited. This affected the kind of music written. Instruments like the clarinet only came into standard use towards the end of the 18th century. Again Mozart took advantage of the new possibilities to write some of his last, and greatest, work for that instrument.

A further significant development was the publication of a new kind of instruction manual aimed at teaching playing techniques to the emerging amateur market. C P E Bach (son of the more famous Johann Sebastian Bach) wrote in 1753 his *Essay on the True Art of Playing the Keyboard*, which was to become a standard textbook for three quarters of a century afterwards. It was contemporary with similar tutors by Quantz for the flute and by Mozart's father, Leopold, for the violin.

Economic matters also affected the kind of music written and played. The size of most orchestras was much smaller than most modern performances use. Composers of the 18th century often bemoaned the fact that the musical forces at their disposal were insufficient. Mozart, for instance, was delighted when in Paris he found an orchestra of a much bigger size than he was used to having, and especially wrote one of his symphonies accordingly (his *Paris Symphony* No 31). Only the biggest cities and wealthiest courts could afford to employ large numbers of professional musicians on any kind of permanent basis. This again affected the work written at a time when most work was written for immediate performance at a specific occasion. Composers, though, were quick to seize on chance possibilities. Visiting horn players, for instance, were exploited by Haydn in one of his symphonies (No 31, the *Horn Signal*). Many players had to double on various instruments during a performance, putting down the violin and taking up the trumpet as necessary.

The general effect of all these changes was a gradual evolution in the social role of both music and musicians. Music became more secular and less tied to the institutions of the ruling orders. Musicians and composers emerged from being essentially feudal servants, and began to become bourgeois professionals with the possibility of working and living as such. The process was by no means complete and was full of contradictory tendencies. The easiest way to grasp it is to look at Mozart's own career, as it embodies many of the general features of the period in extreme form.

From feudal servant to independent musician

Mozart started his career as a child prodigy, paraded around Europe by his father for the entertainment of the rich and famous. His father, Leopold, came from a family of bookbinders and started his adult life as a student of law. He soon abandoned this in favour of music, entering service in Salzburg Cathedral as a musician and valet. His musical talent meant he progressed to become a senior musical official—deputy kapellmeister—in the service of the Prince-Archbishop of Salzburg. Leopold was an accomplished musician himself. He wrote more than 25 symphonies and numerous sacred and instrumental works. His greatest fame was as the author of a manual on violin playing—published the year of Wolfgang's birth—which was widely translated and reprinted several times.

Very soon after Wolfgang's birth his father turned his energies to fostering his son's musical talent. His only other child to survive childhood, Mozart's sister Nannerl, was also musically talented. Leopold trained his children and was soon parading them around the courts of Europe like performing monkeys. When Mozart was just six years old he and his sister played in Munich before the important Elector Maximilien Joseph III. The fame of the gaudily dressed young children performing musical wonders and tricks spread, and the same year they played in front of the imperial court at Vienna. The rest of Mozart's childhood was to be taken up with a series of sweeps around Europe. As well as playing before courts and aristocratic households with a view to winning favour, patronage and a possible later permanent position, Leopold would advertise his prodigious children in public concerts where people would pay to come and watch them perform. France, England, Holland, Germany and Italy were all taken in. By the time he was in his teens Mozart had played in front of most of the important rulers of Europe.

Contemporary accounts make it clear his talent was remarkable. The young Mozart played the keyboard and violin with party tricks like playing blindfold and improvisations thrown in. On his travels he also absorbed the various musical styles of the day. This absorption and then synthesis and creative reworking of a wide variety of musical styles is a key fact underlying Mozart's later music. His phenomenal musical memory helped in this process. In 1770 Mozart heard a performance in St Peter's in Rome of a sacred choral work forbidden to be taken out of the Vatican (Allegri's *Miserere*) and later wrote out the entire fairly long piece from memory. Mozart's travels won him fame, and awards like the papal insignia he received along with a private papal audience in Rome in 1770.

While still a young child he started composing and publishing his own work. His first violin and piano sonatas were written in Paris at the age of seven, his first symphony in London at the age of eight. Early in his life Mozart showed a particular liking for opera, and as a boy and teenager he wrote several operas which were publicly performed. When just 14 he was commissioned to write a six-hour opera in Milan which was performed to critical acclaim (*Mitridate, Re di Ponto*).

All this time Mozart and his father were on leave from their positions as servants of the Prince-Archbishop of Salzburg. The Archbishop was happy to bask in the reflected glory the child prodigy brought to his statelet. Leopold hoped his son would find the possibility of a permanent salaried position at one of the courts of Europe, and, after an audience with the Empress Maria Theresa in 1773, had hopes of a post at the imperial court itself. He was to be disappointed in this hope, and as the child prodigy began to grow up and the novelty value wore thin the matter of a more secure future as a professional musician arose with increasing urgency.

Meanwhile a new Prince-Archbishop, Count Hieronymous Colleredo, had succeeded back in Salzburg. He was distinctly cooler towards the wanderings of his servants, and wanted them to return to their proper place and duties. Mozart, along with his father, was given a position as a musical official in the new archbishop's court—Konzertmeister and court organist. This entailed a string of duties which Mozart increasingly found tedious, such as writing masses and official music for the cycle of courtly events. Mozart became more and more irked by the restraints imposed on him by his official position. He had already had one sharp run-in with Colleredo in 1777 when he had asked for leave to travel once more. The annoyed ruler sacked both Mozart and his father on the spot. After some suitable grovelling to his lord and master Leopold was taken back, while Mozart headed off to Paris with his mother. Eventually Mozart, finding no other suitable possibilities, returned to Salzburg, and the Prince-Archbishop took him back. Mozart was still deeply unhappy with his status and position as a feudal servant. His private letters make clear his deepening sense of bitterness at the situation and the domination of what he saw as stupid, talentless aristocrats. He wrote to his father, 'The heart ennobles the man; and if I am

7 J Stone, 'Mozart's Opinions and Outlook', in H C Robbins Landon (ed), op cit, p143.

8 Ibid, p144.

9 'Mozart as an Individual', in ibid, p105.

assuredly no Count, I have perhaps more honour in me than many a Count; and lackey or Count as soon as he insults me is a scoundrel'.[7] Later he wrote, and had distributed as a broadsheet, a series of joking riddles and aphorisms which include sentiments like:

If you are a poor numbskull then become a cleric. If you are a rich numbskull then become a [tax] farmer. If you are a noble but poor numbskull then become what you can, for bread. If you are, however, a rich, noble numbskull then become what you will; only not a man of sense.[8]

Matters came to a head in 1781 in Vienna—the year the emperor's reforms really began picking up speed. Colleredo had commanded his musician-servant to attend him on a visit to Vienna. Mozart's treatment left little doubt about his status in the feudal hierarchy. Mozart complained to his father about the humiliating set-up:

At about 12 noon we go to table, our lunch party consists of the two valets, body and soul attendants to His Grace the Herr Controleur...the pastry cook, the two cooks and my modest self...the two valets sit at the head of the table whereas at least I have the honour to be placed above the cooks.[9]

Mozart had had enough and petitioned for his release from his master's service. An angry scene with the count followed, with insults exchanged on all sides. A further row with the Prince-Archbishop's chief chamberlain, in which Mozart denounced Colleredo as an 'arrogant conceited cleric', led to Mozart being literally kicked out with a boot up the backside from the chamberlain.

The feudal servant had broken free and was launched on a precarious existence as an independent musician in Vienna, then at the centre of the Emperor's reforms. He was in a contradictory position which can be illustrated by contrasting him with his great predecessor Haydn and successor Beethoven. Joseph Haydn lived most of his life as a feudal servant. Ludwig van Beethoven managed a reasonably successful existence as an independent musician and composer in the years after the French Revolution. Mozart was halfway between these two worlds, never fully breaking free from one and never really achieving the other. So he battled to earn enough money to live, rejecting the worst restrictions of the old society, while at the same time constantly seeking to secure some post at the imperial court or other such place which could guarantee him a stable income. This contradictory position is in many ways echoed in his music and operas. Apart from a minor position, mainly involving composing dances for the court, towards the very end of his life a decade later, Mozart never again had a permanent salaried position. He was half forced into

10. Murray Perahia with the English Chamber Orchestra, notes to 1981 CBS edition of Mozart's *Piano Concerto No 20 in D Minor*.

this position, but had also been driven there by his own rebellion against his allotted place in the old society.

For the rest of his life Mozart lived by marketing his talents both as composer and performer, and it was to be his most creative period. At first he earned his way principally as a virtuoso piano performer. Mostly he played his own music, and in particular wrote his great piano concertos in which piano and orchestra combine. In fact, he virtually invented this form of music. Fellow musicians marvelled at his performing talent, particularly his ability to spontaneously improvise at length on a given theme, which suggest he could have been at home as a jazz pianist in a different age. In this context, and in the interests of debunking romantic myths, it is worth recalling a remark Mozart made when someone commented how he played without showing any effort: 'I had to labour once in order not to show any labour now'.[10]

His popularity as a performer waned in the later 1780s, which began to cause him increasing financial problems. Though these problems were real, their degree is often grossly exaggerated. The problems were more of an insecure source of income with an unpredictable and irregular flow which was due to his new social situation as an independent musician rather than any absolute poverty. For most of the time he was in

Vienna he had a relatively comfortable income by bourgeois standards and managed to move in wealthy circles. He had periodic financial crises, was forced to move to less expensive apartments, and resorted at the worst points to begging from fellow wealthy Freemasons in desperate, almost hysterical tones. But contrary to some of the mythology his debts were modest even at his death. One study reckons Mozart earned between 2,000 and 6,000 florins a year during his time in Vienna. This may have been well below the income of feudal lords like Haydn's master Prince Esterhazy, with his estimated annual income of 700,000 florins from his 45,000 serfs and 10 million acres. But it was considerably more than the typical fairly well off peasant income of less than 300 florins a year, or even minor officials, professional and traders who typically earned less than 1,000 florins a year.[11]

As well as performing, Mozart had recourse to teaching pupils in order to supplement his income. He was also paid for commissioned compositions from opera and religious works to dances, symphonies and serenades. Most of these, though, earned only one-off payments. There were no royalties, and composers were paid a single lump sum regardless of how many times their work might be performed. It was fairly common practice for composers, including Mozart, to slightly

11 A Steptoe, 'Mozart's Social World', and 'Economics', in H C Robbins Landon (ed), op cit, pp63-65, 129.

rework old pieces and pass them off for sale as new. It was also fairly common for lesser musicians to borrow or steal and pass off as their own other people's compositions. It used to be thought this was the true story of the composition of Mozart's brilliant and powerful but unfinished *Requiem Mass*. The mass, it was said, was commissioned by an unknown stranger who sent a messenger with various payments to Mozart. Mozart never finished the *Requiem* due to his own death while working on it. This tragic circumstance has since been worked up into various myths about the approach of Mozart's own death. It is no doubt possible that as Mozart sickened in the last weeks of his life all sorts of psychological feelings connected with the coincidence that he happened to be just then working on a requiem mass may have filled his head and even affected the music—which does have an immense power. The poignancy of the story was increased by the idea that the stranger was in fact a minor aristocrat who intended to pass off Mozart's work as his own. Now the truth appears to be far more straightforward. The commission does not seem to have been anonymous at all, but from Count Walsegg-Stuppach, one of Mozart's fellow Freemasons, whose wife had died. The Count was in the habit of holding concerts at his castle at which works by various composers were played and the audience were then invited to guess the author.

On the subject of myths it is also worth pointing out the degree of censorship that came after Mozart's death as bourgeois circles tried to create a romantic hero, a clean Mozart. In part this was a product of a systematic attempt to use this image of Mozart as a symbol of growing German nationalism in the 19th century. His widow, Constanze, censored some of his more earthy and sexually explicit letters. The words of some of Mozart's many humorous or bawdy songs were also systematically censored. One example, of many, will suffice. One of Mozart's works which for generations was thought to consist of harmless sentiments like, 'Nothing refreshes me more than wine', was actually in the original, 'Lick my arse beautifully, really clean, lick it! That's an oily desire, it's only good smeared with butter' (Mozart had what could be described as an extreme anal fixation throughout most of his life). The faces on various upper class stuffed shirts in London's Royal Festival Hall when the original was performed in 1990 for the first time in two centuries must alone have been worth the entry price!

Classical music, sonata form and the symphony

As well as the changing role of music and musicians in society, the nature of music itself underwent profound changes in the course of the 18th century. New forms of music were developed which have come to be synonymous with classical music ever since. At the centre of this was the evolution of what is called sonata form. To understand what this was about it is necessary to set it against the style of music that preceded it. This is generally labelled baroque music.

Baroque music can, at the risk of oversimplification, be characterised by a number of related elements. Firstly it was based on the 'doctrine of affections'. This meant that once a piece of music started it tended to move at a fairly even pace throughout, without sudden contrasts or changes in tempo. It tended to be based on extending, spinning out and sequentially reproducing or repeating units or phrases of music, a seamless web. In particular the music tended to be based on giving a treble (higher pitch) and bass (lower pitch) line of music roughly equal importance. The two lines moved independently, related by the sophisticated development of a technique called counterpoint (the name derives from the running against each other of two lines of notes when the music is written down). The bass part moved equally with the top part instead of seeking to anchor it. The harmonic and chordal texture was typically filled in and often improvised on a keyboard such as a harpsichord. Baroque music, even when moving quickly, tends to give a feeling of solemnity and grandeur. Once started, a baroque piece of music tends to generate its own momentum and structure, pursuing its course fairly smoothly until its end. As can be imagined, this kind of music fits well with a social reality dominated by seemingly timeless, ordered and god-given institutions such as the church, the whole feudal hierarchy and absolute monarchs.

In the course of the 18th century this baroque style of music was replaced by a very different approach. In its earlier phase in the mid-18th century it was labelled the 'galant' style, and later the classical style. Again the main characteristics can be summed up in a few points. Firstly there was the emergence of a strong melodic line in the treble with a decidedly subservient bass. The treble was supported and the music given texture by realising its chordal, harmonic implications. In the 18th century the modern theory of harmony was first fully developed, above all by French musician Jean-Phillippe Rameau in his *Traité de l'Harmonie* in 1772.

This emergence of the melody was an artistic

echo of the emergence of the individual characteristic of the growing bourgeois society as against the dissolving of the individual into a rigidly ordered society. It paralleled, for example, similar developments in the novel in the 18th century. Alongside this came the abandonment of the doctrine of affections. There was a growing emphasis on shifts of mood and tempo, with contrasts and tension becoming more and more deliberately contrived. Music also became increasingly based on periodic musical phrases and fragments broken up and contrasted rather than simply spun out and repeated in various guises. The kind of periods and rhythms were often derived from dance forms, so you get the appearance of a minuet movement in a multi-part musical work like a symphony, for example. A key technical problem, though, is that this style of music, unlike much baroque music, does not tend to generate its own movement and structure. It requires a structure imposed on it to develop it into music of any length and weight.

Underpinning the whole development was a growing emphasis on an elegance of structure and simplicity of expression based on ideals of classical antiquity from ancient Greece and Rome. Classical proportion and elegance replaced the seamless and complex spinning of baroque counterpoint. This classical emphasis had been seen earlier in the art of the Renaissance and flowered again in the Enlightenment.

Within the stress on classical elegance and structure there was a growing emphasis on tension, dramatic contrast and shifts in mood, tempo and feeling. A combination of order and change, drama and dynamism, but confined within an overall structure, was in many ways a reflection of the dominant feeling of the Enlightenment and the aspirations of the emerging bourgeoisie. All of these were tendencies—the full development can only be seen by contrasting the full development of baroque with classical music. Throughout the 18th century musical forms combined continuity with, as well as a break from, baroque. One of the interesting features of much of Mozart's music, in fact, is how he both stretches the new to its limits at various points and yet continually falls back on the old forms, as in his last work, the *Requiem*, which at points has strong elements of baroque convention.

The resolution of the problem of structure, referred to above, was the use of contrast and tension between differing musical keys and thematic fragments. An aside is necessary to indicate what this involves. If you imagine a piano keyboard, it is divided into black and white notes. Between each successive note, whether black or white, is the same musical interval—a semitone. Most

12 For a brief discussion of this see the preface to the excellent W Mellers, *The Sonata Principle* (London, 1988).

Western music up to the start of the 20th century, until the 'atonal' revolution associated with figures like Schoenberg, was tonal. This is based on the music being founded on a selection of seven of the possible notes in an octave—which is divided into 12 semitones. There are various possible selections, but the dominant forms which came to be used in Western music were based on selections known as major and minor scales.

The key of a piece of music is the scale it is based on. So C major is all the white notes of the piano, G major has one black note in each set of seven, and so on. Keys can be closely related or more distant. Minor keys are distinguished from major ones in a variety of ways, the most crucial, but not the only one, being a flattened interval between the first and third note of the scale, ie the interval between these two notes being one semitone lower than in a major scale. Though not always true, major scales tend to give a lighter and at times majestic feeling, while minor keys often give a feeling of sadness, or unease and tension. This is rooted in very material facts such as whether the ratio between the vibrations associated with notes is in a simple or more complex ratio, and also certain factors to do with the properties of the human voice.[12] It is of course not reducible to such factors, as the impression a piece of music makes is also decisively conditioned by social and psychological factors, and so generalisations about the feelings created by major and minor keys should be used with some care—it is perfectly possible to write a bright piece of music in a minor key and a sad one in a major key!

The crucial point in the development of classical music in the 18th century was the way shifts between different keys and contrasts between differing thematic fragments were used to sustain a dramatic tension and impose a structure on a piece of music. The move from one key to another is typically marked by a cadence, a decisive punctuation of the music. Movements between different keys had long been used in music before the classical age, but their systematic use in this way was a new element.

Classical form, then, is based on a melodic line with strong chordal harmonic underpinning, broken into phrases and fragments. It has an overall structure which aimed to be elegant and classical in proportion. But within this there is a development by a series of contrasts between different thematic fragments and between different keys. This typically creates development and drama that proceeds through the systematic use of, and working out of, contrast and contradiction. The tension is often resolved by a final move back to the dominant key of the whole piece.

Sonata form was a style based on this approach and which in outline, though rarely followed rigidly or precisely, came to dominate the structure of much classical music in the late 18th and throughout the 19th century. It is a form in which single movements of multi-part works like symphonies or concertos can be written. A movement in sonata form is made up of three distinct sections known as the exposition, development and recapitulation (the names giving a fairly accurate description of the purpose of each). Within this structure different themes, musical ideas or fragments are linked and developed through the kind of process described above. The emergence of sonata form triumphantly solved the problem of how to create music on a large scale with an overall structure and unity out of small melodic fragments, and with contrast and drama built into it.

The most important of the new forms developed in the 18th century was the symphony. This has come to be, for many, almost synonymous with classical music, and is certainly its most 'public' face. The origins of the symphony lie in Italian opera. Before the action started there would be a musical overture, setting the scene for what was to follow. Typically this was a short piece of music in three movements, a moderately fast opening, a slow centre, and either a fast finale or a dance-like minuet. Gradually this became developed into longer pieces of music, and increasingly overtures became played both in the theatre and the concert room. Very often composers, including Mozart, would adapt overtures to dramatic works into purely musical concert symphonies. Symphonies became longer, and composers often experimented with both the number and order of movements. In Austria a four-movement symphony grew and later came to dominate (with fast, slow, minuet and fast movements, usually in that order). Within this variety the typical pattern was for movements to be written in sonata form.

At first symphonies tended to be mainly in major keys, but after about 1760 minor key symphonies or works exploiting the contrasting of minor with major keys became more common, and the symphony's expressive power was thereby considerably enriched. In the 1770s many composers, including Haydn and Mozart, went through a period labelled Sturm und Drang (Storm and Stress), a name derived from a German literary movement, though the musical movement largely preceded the literary one. This led to a deliberate heightening of the dramatic intensity of the music, often using minor keys. Haydn's symphonies in this period often have descriptive titles like *La Passione*. One example is

13 Ibid, p617.
14 Ibid, p589.

Haydn's G minor symphony No 39. Another is Mozart's G minor symphony No 25, with its 'passionate repeated notes and brusque changes of dynamics'.[13]

An enormous number of symphonies were written, mainly by lesser known composers. The most important figure in the first half of the 18th century was the Bohemian Johann Stamnitz. He worked for both the wealthy French financier and bourgeois La Riche de la Pouplinière and the feudal ruler the Elector Palatine at Mannheim in Germany. At Mannheim, Stamnitz had the luxury of working with perhaps the finest and largest orchestra of the day, thanks to the patronage of the elector. In his hands the symphony became more and more divorced from its operatic origins, and developed into a form of music in its own right. The size and professionalism of the Mannheim orchestra were renowned throughout Europe, with powerful musical effects known as 'Mannheim sky-rockets' and the 'Mannheim steamroller' a speciality. One music historian sums up Stamnitz and the Mannheim orchestra:

Stamnitz vigorously expressed the feelings of a growing public which had been unrepresented in the aristocratic art of the previous generation. The bourgeois forces in the Age of Enlightenment knew that the future was with them. Their self-confidence is reflected in the jaunty vitality of Stamnitz's music.[14]

Joseph Haydn developed the symphony further, writing 104 numbered ones in his long life. Again, the link between the new music and the changing and increasingly bourgeois society was well understood by contemporaries. To quote the same historian as above:

The growth of 18th century sonata style is the musical expression of...new democracy. Indeed, the symphony orchestra itself reflected a democratic ideal; Joseph von Holzmeister, in a speech delivered on the occasion of Haydn's admission to the Masonic Order, pointed out that Haydn had created a new order in the orchestra, 'for if every instrument did not consider the rights and properties and the other instruments, in addition to its own rights, if it did not often diminish its own volume in order not to do damage to the utterance of its companions, the end—which is beauty—would not be attained.[15]

Mozart drew on both the rich orchestration of Mannheim and Haydn's work, combined with a synthesis of a host of lesser composers. His early symphonies, like much of his early work, are technically brilliant but little different to countless others of the period. But in his mature symphonies, especially the last three (39, 40, 41), written in Vienna in the heady decade of the 1780s and Josephinian reform, he wrote what still remain some of the finest examples of this form of music. Some of the technical aspects of these works (such as the use of certain

15 Ibid, p586.

16 Ibid, p626.
17 Ibid, p596.

keys and the emphasis on woodwind) are linked with Masonic ritual and Mozart's Masonic beliefs. This has led some to see in them 'the affirmations about life and death which he had embodied in his emotional reinterpretation of Freemasonry...a musical expression of what he had discovered to be his religion'.[16]

If the symphony was the most important development in the 'public' face of music in the 18th century, this was paralleled by the invention of another new form—the string quartet. The origins of the string quartet (for two violins, viola and cello) were somewhat different from what it later became:

The birth of the string quartet was once more a democratic process; music moved not merely from church and court to the chamber or living room, but even into the streets. Vienna was a-jingle with serenading parties playing in the open air.[17]

This affected the style of the music. It had to be fairly simple, with recognisable tunes and rhythms, and rudimentary accompaniment—it was hardly practical to carry a piano or harpsichord around!

Later Haydn, virtually single-handed, transformed the form into something more profound—significantly during his Storm and Stress period of the 1770s. He began to write for each instrument in the quartet as an independent entity, and evolved a deeper, more musically complex style not suited to open air 'band' performance. Haydn's quartets become 'a dialogue of "four sensible people conversing with one another"'.[18]

Mozart was to write some important quartets, heavily influenced by, and some of which he dedicated to, Haydn. The 'dramatic dialogue' between the four instruments creates music which one commentator notes has a 'frightening quality', but one which 'is inseparable from its restraint. It is devoid of rhetoric, yet more dramatic music has never been created'.[19]

If the symphony was a reflection of the public face of the new music and the self-confidence of the bourgeoisie, the string quartet evolved to become the more intimate private face. It has since typically been used as the form in which composers express more private feelings and thoughts, often in densely argued musical terms, compared to the more public sentiments and appearance of symphonic scale works.

One of the forms of music to survive, at least in name, the 18th century shift towards the new classical style was that of the concerto—a solo instrument with an orchestral accompaniment. This is the form of works like Vivaldi's famous *Four Seasons* for solo violin and orchestra, published in 1725. In part the concerto survived through the potential it offered for virtuoso display. It

18 Ibid, p601.
19 Ibid, p620.

59

had originated in improvised solo display, but it had been 'a not very taxing display piece for a soloist with instrumental accompaniment. It whiled away idle moments with a pleasing euphony'.[20] This is an overly harsh judgement of some of the great pre-classical concertos, like Vivaldi's, but it is fair to say that Mozart wrote some distinguished concertos which in many ways do fall in the category of pleasing but fairly shallow works—such as his *Flute and Harp Concerto*.

However, Mozart transformed the nature of the concerto when he turned to write his great piano concertos. He wrote 27 numbered concertos and at least the last nine, written for his own performance in Vienna, are masterpieces unique in the history of music. They are built round a dramatic argument between piano and orchestra with the most powerful first movements written in sonata form. They contain shifting moods of light and dark, and in works like the D minor concerto (No 20) disturbing, jagged pulsating rhythms. The music is no longer simply meant to entertain or impress, but rather to have a strong emotional effect on listeners. Mozart's work:

...sees the piano concerto as a duality in unity...it offered an allegorical expression of the separation of the individual (soloist) from society (the orchestra). But this separation is made in order that the soloist and the orchestra can, in the course of

the music, evolve a new relationship. The Mozartian concerto threatens, only in order to vindicate civilisation.[21]

21 Ibid.
22 Ibid, p600.

Few composers afterwards have even tried to match Mozart's achievement in these works. They have a unique balance, avoiding either the piano simply being subordinated to the orchestra, or the orchestra being simply a background to a display of virtuosity by the soloist.

Mozart's mature instrumental music was a product of a revolution in musical style that occurred in the 18th century. He developed aspects of this new style farther than anyone else, and in doing so wrote some music which has a power rarely equalled since. Yet at the same time he was constantly falling back on old conventions and styles. It is this shifting and uneasy mix of the old, the conventional, the new and the unexpected in his music, in many ways paralleling his own situation and the society in which he lived, which is perhaps the strongest characteristic of Mozart's music. The particular power of Mozart's best music is captured by one musicologist:

One finds this precariousness: the sudden defeat of expectation, the interruption of a norm of behaviour, whether of tonality or of melodic, harmonic or rhythmic formula. One does not usually find this quality in composers who lived before the Age of Reason, in an age of Faith, whether in God or the State.[22]

A new kind of opera

Mozart saw himself principally as an opera composer, and it is in this field that his greatest artistic achievements lie. He could not write as many operas as he wanted. Opera was, and is, a fairly expensive business to produce, and therefore composers had usually to rely on opportunities presented by commissions from those with sufficient wealth to make them.

The origins of opera lie in the Renaissance attempt to rediscover the heights of the culture of classical antiquity. In music this took place between about 1425 and 1600. For a variety of technical reasons a Florentine scholar in the late 16th century called Girolamo Mei concluded that the great plays of ancient Greek writers like Aeschylus, Sophocles and Euripides were actually sung works accompanied by music (a conclusion which has since been disputed). This gave birth to opera, partly in France but mainly in Italy.

By the 18th century opera, dominated by Italy, had evolved into two quite distinct styles. These were known as *opera seria* and *opera buffa*, or serious and comic opera. *Opera seria* was unashamedly elitist. Its plots were loosely based on ancient history or mythology. Its characters, drawn from the ruling class, were an endless parade of kings and generals. In the 18th century the central figure in dictating the stories and words used (in opera called the libretto) was the poet Pietro Metastasio. He was the Caesarian poet at the imperial court in Vienna—a post somewhat more important than the poet laureate in Britain today. He banned comedy and distorted ancient history where needed to write librettos flattering to the ruling classes he served. So the upper class heroes and heroines drawn from ancient history were given attributes like steadfastness, loyalty and generosity which were meant to portray a nobility of character. The aim was straightforward. As one commentator notes, 'The intention was to bolster the position of the contemporary upper class by demonstrating on stage its worthiness to rule'.[23]

Mozart wrote several *opera seria*—some, like *Idomeneo* and *La Clemenza di Tito* (*The Clemency of Titus*), are better than normal examples of the form. But fairly lifeless propaganda on behalf of the decaying ruling order is perhaps the most accurate way to sum up *opera seria*. The role of *opera seria* had an impact on its structure and musical form. It was backed by the ruling class and financially well supported. It therefore tended to attract the most technically gifted singers, and soon came to have vocal lines demanding virtuosity in technique,

23 M Robinson, 'The origins of Mozart's style: Opera', in H C Robbins Landon (ed), op cit, p74.

63

with plenty of opportunities to show off. Incidentally, it also used and depended on the adult male soprano, literally the *castrato*!

All this meant that *opera seria* was singers' opera. It was largely based on a succession of lengthy set piece solo numbers or arias. And these were usually in a form, called *da capo*, in which the first half of a two-part song was repeated with assorted vocal gymnastics and showy embellishments added. Again, this tended to work against any interaction between the characters. There was little real conflict or drama, and the form of the arias tended to break up and halt movement and development in the drama. The music and drama became subordinate to the demands of the singers. Each singer had a set number of arias depending on their place in the pecking order—four or five for the leading singer, perhaps one for the least important.

Opera seria underwent a process of reform in the 18th century associated with the musician Christoph Gluck in his operas *Orpheus and Euridice* and then *Alceste* in the 1760s. He attacked the worst aspects of *opera seria*. He argued that music should support the drama, not interrupt it with over-ornate embellishments. Gluck was against the *da capo* aria with its repeated first section, and argued for a simplicity of style in the whole structure of opera.

The real change in opera, though, originated not with the reform of *opera seria* but in the other main tradition, *opera buffa* (comic opera).

Opera buffa was based on satirising certain qualities, such as incredulity, miserliness and lechery, held by the upper classes to be typical of the lower classes. It therefore consisted of exclusively middle and lower class characters like servants. Often *opera buffa* would be served up as two comic interludes between the three acts of an *opera seria*, thus underlining, in the eyes of the ruling order, the separation between their world and its qualities, and that of the lower orders. They could bask in the reflected glory of the noble characters in the *opera seria* and then laugh at the inferior quality of those beneath them in society in between courses.

By the mid-18th century, however, *opera buffa* underwent a change. This was in large part an artistic reflection of the growing importance of the bourgeoisie and the undermining of the existing social structure that was occurring. *Opera buffa* began to enlarge its cast of characters, even including figures drawn from the lower ranks of the aristocracy. This mixing together of different social groups opened up a whole new range of possibilities. It led to the crossing and blurring of the old dividing lines between what were considered proper qualities of different social groups. Ordinary human characteristics become increasingly portrayed instead of, or rather mixed with, the old stock stereotypes. Musically the development produced a number of effects. The unnatural *castrati* were dropped, and more important parts were given to the bass voice, which had dropped out of currency. In general the greater range of characters in *opera buffa* meant a greater musical variety was introduced. Also, because the best technical singers were engaged in *opera seria*, the parts in *opera buffa* were often sung by singers with more moderate vocal skills. It tended, therefore, to be less showy and possess simpler tunes. It had, above all, much more interaction between the different characters, and was less rigid and dead than *opera seria*. Real drama and action could develop. This was embodied in the growth of the ensemble, in which all the cast would sing together at the end of each act. The number of ensembles grew as the number of arias fell.

It was out of these developments that Mozart was to break new ground by creating in his greatest operas real musical theatre, where words and music combine to create a marvellous whole in a way no opera had ever done before. Mozart did not completely break from the old traditions. He continued to angle right to the end of his life for commissions for *opera seria*. Indeed his last opera, *The Clemency of Titus*, is in that form. Nevertheless he also stepped radically forward in the great operas he wrote in the 1780s during his Viennese decade in collaboration with the librettist Lorenzo da Ponte: *Le Nozze di Figaro* (*The Marriage of Figaro*), *Don Giovanni* and *Cosi Fan Tutte* (*All Women Behave That Way*), and Mozart's Masonic opera, *Die Zauberflöte* (*The Magic Flute*).

A word about Da Ponte would be useful, as his words and story are a central part of the operas' power. He was born near Venice as Emmanuele Conegliano in 1749, the son of a Jewish tanner and leather dealer. He converted to Christianity and thereupon adopted the name of the bishop in the area he was born in. He studied in a Catholic seminary, which prepared people to become priests. He took his holy orders and eventually moved to Venice, where he ended up as professor of rhetoric at a seminary. However, his ideas grew increasingly radical. In 1774 he had to recite a poem at an annual official event. He took as his subject, 'Whether Man is Happier in an Organised Society or in a Simple State of Nature'. This notion, derived from the works of the philosopher Jean Jacques Rousseau, was anathema to those who were very happy with the current organised society, notably the church, the aristocracy and the state.

Da Ponte was promptly sacked and banned from holding any teaching post. On top of this came his breaking of the sexual rules of society, in particular an affair with a married woman from an upper class family, which proved the final straw. He was banished from Venice and eventually ended up in Vienna in the throes of Joseph II's liberal reforms. It was there that he met and collaborated with Mozart. In 1791, as Joseph's reforms were being sharply curtailed, Da Ponte once again found himself the subject of official attacks. Yet again he was banished, and after a series of travels ended up in the US, where he became a revered and respectable academic, known in that country as 'the father of Italian studies', before dying at the ripe old age of 90.

The Marriage of Figaro is a revolutionary opera in more than one sense. It was based on the play of the same name by the French dramatist Beaumarchais. It is the story of how an aristocrat trying to revive his old feudal sexual claims on the bodies of his women vassals and servants about to be married, the *droit de seigneur*, is outwitted and foiled by his servant Figaro, Figaro's fellow servant and bride to be Susannah, and the Count's wife. The original play is fiercely anti-aristocratic and anti-feudal. The sexual politics of *The Marriage of Figaro* are also fairly radical, with central and powerful roles for the two leading women, and a sexually ambiguous role for a young adolescent servant page called Cherubino. This character constantly disturbs the sexual stability of the other roles, and continually flirts with and tries to seduce the other women including the Countess (in a sequel play by Beaumarchais the Countess has an illegitimate child by the young servant). It is both biting satire against central aspects of the existing social order and very funny. For that reason Beaumarchais' play was temporarily banned by the ruling orders in France, but still prohibited from being performed in Vienna in the 1780s. Napoleon later claimed that the play, first performed in 1784, was an important stage in the development of the French Revolution. This is an exaggeration, but the play was certainly a very sharp artistic expression of the contradictions eating away at the old society which would soon burst forth in revolution. The French King Louis XVI is reputed to have said that for the play to be performed in public the Bastille would have to be demolished first. He later relented, but the point was to prove prophetic.

The play, though banned from performance, was, however, available in Vienna in printed form. That Mozart proposed to Da Ponte to write an opera based on this play was an act of some daring and defiance, as the reputation of the play was well known. In the resulting

24 *The Marriage of Figaro* (John Calder, with English National Opera and the Royal Opera, London, 1983), libretto, p112.

In all cases of quotes from opera librettos I have given the English translation used in the English National Opera guides and generally used in performances there.

25 Preface by Da Ponte in ibid, p46.

opera much of the overt politics is watered down compared to the play, though not the sexual politics. So a long tirade against aristocratic privilege by Figaro is cut, yet a speech by one woman character is partially retained which includes sentiments like, 'Surely all women ought to support one another/When we think of how we're treated'.[24] And the women and the sexually disturbing Cherubino remain at the centre of the drama and provide the central and strongest characters. The opera was only performed thanks to Da Ponte's successful efforts in persuading the Emperor Joseph that the offensive parts of the play had been cut.

Musically and dramatically it is quite different to any opera previously produced. Firstly, it is very amusing, even when seen today. Secondly, the unprecedented emphasis on ensembles rather than static arias means that the action and drama move with a new intensity, and the interaction between the characters means they become more fully rounded and human compared to the wooden stereotypes of most previous operas. There are even musical parodies within *Figaro* of several of the conventions of *opera seria*. It was with some justification that Da Ponte could claim it was 'a new type of spectacle'.[25]

The music is some of the finest ever written by Mozart and weaves together with the words to create musical theatre of the highest order. One critic notes, 'The music is literally progressive...in that it is built so that it never relaxes, because each phrase is always pressing forward into the next,' and, 'the way the music proceeds, in fact, is by building up tensions and immediately releasing them, those releases themselves becoming a source for new tensions'.[26]

The politics are not entirely dropped either. Figaro has, for example, a solo number in which he defies his lord and master, singing, 'If you are after/A little amusement/You may go dancing/I'll play the tune/...Yes, Sir, believe me/I'll put a spoke in your/Wheel if I can'.[27] The Count thunders later at the attempts to frustrate his feudal rights and privileges:

Must I forego my pleasure?/While serf of mine rejoices/... No! I'll show you I'm your master/No more will you defy me/Dare you be so presumptuous/As to venture to thwart me?/Dare you, my servant, laugh at me?[28]

The Count's defiance is to no avail, and he is outwitted. However, at the end all the characters are reunited in forgiveness. The social and sexual order, though threatened, is, for now and if fragilely, restored. *Figaro* did not achieve huge popularity in Vienna, where it seems not to have gone down well with the minor aristocracy who recognised themselves in the figure of the thwarted

26 'Music and Comedy in The Marriage of Figaro' in ibid, p31.
27 Ibid, libretto, p52.
28 Ibid, p96.

29 B Brophy, *Mozart the Dramatist* (London, 1988), p129.

Count. It proved immensely popular in the more liberal imperial city of Prague, where Mozart noted with pleasure how the many catchy tunes in *Figaro* were constantly whistled in the streets.

The Prague success of *Figaro* resulted in the city commissioning the second of the Mozart/Da Ponte collaborations, *Don Giovanni*. *Don Giovanni* is quite different to *Figaro*, however. On the surface it is a reworking of the old tale of Don Juan as, for instance, in the 17th century French dramatist Molière's play of that name. A dissolute aristocratic rake, who lives by pursuing sexual conquests of women of any sort, is finally punished and dragged down to hell. The opera retains much of this traditional element in the story—and has as its subtitle 'The Rake Punished'. This has led some commentators to see it as quite different in character to *Figaro*: 'Counter-revolutionary...the manifest meaning of *Don Giovanni* is pro-Christianity and anti-Enlightenment'.[29] This seems to me to entirely miss the point. *Don Giovanni* is fundamentally ambiguous, and it is precisely this ambiguity which gives it its strength.

The opera portrays the reactionary story of a rake punished for his sins by being dragged off to hell in musical terms of immense power, especially in the overture and in the penultimate scene, when the statue of a man killed by Don Giovanni comes to life and drags him off to the eternal flames. These contain music which even today sends a shiver down the spine.

But that is only one side of the drama. The moralistic outward structure of the tale contains contradictory elements. For instance, throughout the opera Don Giovanni fails to make a single sexual conquest despite all his efforts—an overwhelmingly unsuccessful rake if ever there was one. More importantly the opera is dramatically and musically structured to create in direct opposition to the moral tale a deep sympathy and attraction to the Don himself. He refuses to bow down before the moral and sexual conventions of church and society. In one scene, for instance, the words 'Long live liberty' are inflated musically far beyond the requirements of the drama. Significantly these lines were missing from the libretto submitted to the censor in advance of the first performance.

Most tellingly, Don Giovanni throughout hurls defiance at all attempts to make him conform: 'Though the powers of Hell assail me/Let the Day of Judgement threaten/Faithful to myself I'll stay'.[30] In the dramatic scene where he is dragged off to hell this defiance shines through in the words and music. The statue invites the Don to dine with him in eternity. 'No man shall call me a

30 *Don Giovanni* (John Calder, with English National Opera and the Royal Opera, London, 1990), libretto, p79.

31 Ibid, pp103-104.

32 Ibid, p106.

33 J Rushton, *Classical Music* (London, 1986), p72.

coward/I have resolved, I'll go', he answers. The statue, transparently representing the established order, thunders, 'Penitence still can save you/Or face the final sentence'. The Don ripostes, 'No, I despise repentance/Off with you, leave my sight!' 'Pentinence' the statue demands once more. Yet even as he is hauled into hell Don Giovanni refuses to submit and returns a final defiant 'No!'[31]

After this scene the opera ends with a moral chorus involving the other characters declaiming, 'Sinners end as they begin'.[32] But this, after the power and music of the previous scene, simply underlines the deep ambiguity at the heart of the whole opera. As one commentator asks, 'Is *Don Giovanni* a Catholic opera, a symbol of revolution with a hero at war with his class, or a celebration of sexuality?'[33] *Don Giovanni* is all these at once, and this is what makes it great drama and art.

Finally let me turn to Mozart's Masonic opera, *The Magic Flute*. This was written in late 1790 and early 1791 after the death of Joseph II and the ending of his reforms, and just as reaction was really picking up force under the new emperor who was soon to go to war against revolutionary France. Freemasonry was under attack for its close association with the enlightened reforms. Yet in these circumstances Mozart chose to write an opera which is a fairly open defence of Freemasonry, and its stress on reason and enlightenment.

At one level the work is musically brilliant. But it is almost a pantomime and was often played at this level, with special effects and jokes, often improvised, both dramatic and musical. On one occasion Mozart himself threw the cast into confusion by playing unscheduled from the wings. The opera was not performed in the main theatres in Vienna but in the more popular Theater auf der Wieden in the suburbs. It seems to have attracted huge audiences of a distinctly more popular composition than was typical of the day. The theatre was run by Mozart's friend and fellow Mason Emanuel Schikaneder, who also wrote the bulk of the libretto.

Throughout the opera there is a more serious undertone alongside the pantomime, which at times comes to dominate. The story is complex and at times contradictory. A young prince is sent by the Queen of the Night to rescue her daughter, who has been kidnapped by the evil high priest of a wicked secret order. The prince is given a magic flute to protect himself. The secret order turns out to be the Brotherhood of Reason. The Queen of the Night is transformed and revealed to be the real evil character. Eventually after undergoing several ordeals the prince and princess are united and

34 W Mellers, op cit, p729.
35 B Brophy, op cit, p197.

together undergo initiation into the brotherhood. The Queen of the Night is defeated. Reason is triumphant.

The Queen of the Night symbolises reaction, and is a fairly obvious representation of the old anti-Masonic Empress Maria Theresa and the Catholic church. The prince, Tamino, moves from a blind faith in her to an illumination which leads him to join the Brotherhood of Reason. Some commentators push the connection of the opera to contemporary events further, suggesting Tamino is the recently deceased enlightened Emperor Joseph II (conveniently putting to one side his turn to reaction at the end of his reign) and the princess, Pamina, the Austrian people, and so on.[34]

What is true is that whole opera is full of Masonic symbolism. Sarastro, the high priest of the Temple of Reason, sings of 'this holy Masonry'. In the music, the use of certain keys and intervals and song forms is also closely tied to Masonic ritual and symbolism: 'The metaphor of light bursting through darkness underlies and shapes the whole story'.[35] In the context of political events of 1791 this stress, and the opera's popularity, was not one which would have pleased the increasingly reactionary authorities. Mozart, however, died only two months after completing the opera.

The opera also tackles head on a subject of debate

within Freemasonry itself. The bulk of Masonic lodges were notoriously anti-women. The Temple of Reason in the opera and the all-male priests repeat such sentiments over and over again, insisting that a woman needs a man to guide her. Yet at the end Mozart and Schikaneder turn all this on its head. The heroine, Pamina, joins the order alongside Tamino after undergoing the same initiation ordeals. Moreover it is she who leads the way and guides Tamino. 'I myself will lead you', she declares as Tamino balks at the 'gates of terror'.[36] This was a message the bulk of Masons would not have been very happy to hear.

The opera concludes when 'wickedness is banished and superstition overcome by the rising sun of wisdom. It is perhaps the fullest artistic expression of the Enlightenment'.[37]

36 Ibid, p164.
37 J Rushton, op cit, p74.

Conclusion

I have tried to show how Mozart was a creation of a society in transition, one which was riddled with contradictions, and undergoing profound and soon to be revolutionary change.

This is not to deny he was a musical genius, but simply to stress that neither he nor his music can be understood without seeing them against the background of the changing society and the musical revolution of which they were a product. In his best work Mozart expressed in art aspects of and contradictions in these processes, and much more besides. He and his work remain today among the highest points in the history of art.

In the years after Mozart, many of the musical developments which figures like Haydn and Mozart had taken to their highest point would be deepened and transformed in a revolutionary manner again by Ludwig van Beethoven. He was a composer who, writing in the aftermath of the French Revolution, was, unlike Mozart, a conscious bourgeois revolutionary. Beethoven saw his music as representing, heralding and celebrating a new bourgeois society—in words this is clearly expressed in the *Ode to Joy* (*Freedom*) which forms the text to the final movement of his famous *Ninth Symphony*.

38 W Mellers, op cit, pxii.

Mozart was not in this position. His music and operas are rooted in the contradiction between the decaying old society which has yet to die and the growing new society yet to be born. It is an uneasy and shifting balance between 'acceptance and protest, tradition and revolution, lyricism and tonal drama'.[38] It is this which in many ways gives them their particular and unique power. The opera *Figaro* aptly symbolises Mozart's position. The old order is threatened, even undermined and defeated at points. But at the end the triumph turns back into reconciliation and the maintenance, albeit on a very fragile basis, of the existing order.

Yet as Mozart died the world was playing out a very different ending. The overture had closed, and the curtain had lifted on a Parisian drama in which Figaros in the mass were not only defying their lords and masters, but would soon bury them and their society for ever.

For other publications from Redwords go to:
www.redwords.org.uk